SUDAN COOKBOOK

Traditional Recipes from Sudan

LIAM LUXE

Copyright © 2024 Liam Luxe

All rights reserved.

CONTENTS

INTRODUCTION

This cookbook is all about sharing delicious recipes from Sudan –
a place with lots of different cultures and traditions that make its
food super special.

Sudan is like a big pot where lots of different flavors come
together. The recipes in this book are like secret family recipes that
have been passed down for a long time. They're made to be easy
for anyone to try, whether you're a kitchen pro or just starting out.

In these pages, you'll find simple and authentic recipes that let
you bring a bit of Sudanese magic into your own kitchen. The
food in Sudan is a mix of tasty spices, yummy herbs, and cool
ways of cooking that make it unique.

This cookbook is here to help you have fun in the kitchen.
Whether you want to make something special, try new flavors, or
just enjoy cooking, you'll love making and eating these Sudanese
dishes.

Happy cooking!

BREAKFAST DELIGHTS

FUL MEDAMES (FAVA BEANS STEW)

- **Servings:** 4
- **Time:** 30 minutes

Ingredients:

- 2 cups cooked fava beans
- 2 cloves garlic, minced
- 1 tomato, chopped
- 1/4 cup olive oil
- 1 teaspoon cumin
- Salt, to taste
- Fresh parsley, for garnish
- Lemon wedges, for serving

Instructions:

1. Heat olive oil in a pan.
2. Add minced garlic and sauté until golden.
3. Add chopped tomatoes and cook until soft.
4. Stir in cooked fava beans, cumin, and salt.
5. Mash some beans with a fork for thickness.
6. Cook for 10 minutes, stirring occasionally.
7. Garnish with fresh parsley.
8. Serve hot with lemon wedges.

KISRA (SUDANESE FLATBREAD)

- **Servings:** 8
- **Time:** 45 minutes

Ingredients:

- 2 cups sorghum flour
- 1 cup all-purpose flour
- 1 teaspoon salt
- 2.5 cups water
- 1 tablespoon vegetable oil

Instructions:

1. In a bowl, mix sorghum flour, all-purpose flour, and salt.
2. Gradually add water while stirring to form a smooth batter.
3. Let the batter rest for 15 minutes.
4. Heat a non-stick pan over medium heat.
5. Add vegetable oil to the batter and stir.
6. Pour a ladle of batter onto the pan, spreading it thinly.

7. Cook for 2-3 minutes until the edges lift.
8. Flip and cook the other side until golden.
9. Repeat with the remaining batter.
10. Serve warm and enjoy your Kisra with your favorite toppings.

ASEEDA (SORGHUM PORRIDGE)

- **Servings:** 4
- **Time:** 25 minutes

Ingredients:

- 1 cup sorghum flour
- 3 cups water
- Pinch of salt
- 2 tablespoons honey (optional)
- Nuts or dried fruits for garnish (optional)

Instructions:

1. In a pot, bring water to a boil.
2. In a bowl, mix sorghum flour with a pinch of salt.
3. Gradually add the sorghum mixture to the boiling water, stirring continuously to avoid lumps.
4. Reduce heat and simmer for 15-20 minutes, stirring frequently until it thickens.
5. If desired, add honey for sweetness.
6. Continue cooking until the porridge reaches your desired consistency.
7. Remove from heat and let it cool for a few minutes.
8. Serve warm, garnished with nuts or dried fruits if you like.

SHAIYAH (SUDANESE TEA)

- **Servings:** 2
- **Time:** 15 minutes

Ingredients:

- 2 cups water
- 2 teaspoons loose black tea leaves
- 1 cup whole milk
- 2 tablespoons sugar (adjust to taste)
- 1 cinnamon stick (optional)

Instructions:

1. In a pot, bring water to a boil.
2. Add black tea leaves and let it steep for 5 minutes.
3. Pour in the whole milk and bring the mixture to a gentle simmer.
4. Add sugar to taste and stir until it dissolves.
5. If desired, toss in a cinnamon stick for extra flavor.
6. Simmer for an additional 5 minutes, allowing the flavors to meld.
7. Strain the tea into cups.

BEGHARIYAT (SUDANESE DOUGHNUTS)

- **Servings:** 12
- **Time:** 1 hour

Ingredients:

- 2 cups all-purpose flour

- 1/4 cup sugar
- 1 teaspoon baking powder
- 1/4 teaspoon salt
- 1/2 cup milk
- 2 tablespoons melted butter
- 1 teaspoon vanilla extract
- Vegetable oil for frying
- Powdered sugar for dusting

Instructions:

1. In a bowl, whisk together flour, sugar, baking powder, and salt.
2. Add milk, melted butter, and vanilla extract. Mix until a soft dough forms.
3. On a floured surface, roll the dough to 1/2-inch thickness.
4. Cut out doughnut shapes using a cutter or a glass.
5. Heat vegetable oil in a pan to 350°F (175°C).
6. Fry doughnuts until golden brown, turning once.
7. Drain on paper towels to remove excess oil.
8. Dust with powdered sugar while still warm.
9. Allow to cool slightly before serving.

MULUKHIYAH OMELETTE (JUTE LEAF OMELETTE)

- **Servings:** 2
- **Time:** 20 minutes

Ingredients:

- 4 eggs
- 1 cup chopped mulukhiyah (jute leaves), fresh or frozen

- 1 small onion, finely chopped
- 1 tomato, diced
- Salt and pepper to taste
- 2 tablespoons vegetable oil

Instructions:

1. In a bowl, beat the eggs and season with salt and pepper.
2. Heat vegetable oil in a pan over medium heat.
3. Add chopped onions and sauté until golden.
4. Add diced tomatoes and cook until softened.
5. Add chopped mulukhiyah to the pan and cook for 3-5 minutes.
6. Pour the beaten eggs over the mulukhiyah mixture.
7. Allow the edges to set, then gently lift and tilt the pan to let the uncooked eggs flow to the edges.
8. Once the omelette is mostly set, flip it to cook the other side briefly.
9. Ensure both sides are cooked to your liking.
10. Slide onto a plate and serve hot.

TAMIA (SUDANESE FALAFEL)

- **Servings:** 4
- **Time:** 30 minutes (plus soaking time)

Ingredients:

- 1 cup dried fava beans, soaked overnight
- 1 small onion, chopped
- 2 cloves garlic
- 1 teaspoon ground cumin
- 1 teaspoon ground coriander

- 1/2 teaspoon baking soda
- Salt and pepper to taste
- Vegetable oil for frying

Instructions:

1. Rinse and drain the soaked fava beans.
2. In a food processor, combine fava beans, chopped onion, garlic, cumin, coriander, baking soda, salt, and pepper.
3. Blend until the mixture forms a coarse paste.
4. Transfer the mixture to a bowl and let it rest for 10-15 minutes.
5. Heat vegetable oil in a pan over medium heat.
6. Shape the falafel mixture into small patties.
7. Fry the falafel until golden brown on both sides.
8. Drain on paper towels to remove excess oil.
9. Serve hot with your favorite dipping sauce or in a pita.

EGGPLANT SHAKSHUKA

- **Servings:** 4
- **Time:** 40 minutes

Ingredients:

- 2 large eggplants, diced
- 1 onion, finely chopped
- 2 bell peppers, diced
- 3 cloves garlic, minced
- 1 can (14 oz) diced tomatoes
- 4 eggs
- 1 teaspoon cumin
- 1 teaspoon paprika

- Salt and pepper to taste
- Fresh parsley for garnish
- Olive oil for cooking

Instructions:

1. Heat olive oil in a large pan over medium heat.
2. Add chopped onions and sauté until golden.
3. Add diced eggplants and bell peppers, cook until softened.
4. Stir in minced garlic, cumin, paprika, salt, and pepper.
5. Pour in diced tomatoes with their juice. Simmer for 15 minutes.
6. Make small wells in the tomato mixture and crack an egg into each well.
7. Cover the pan and let the eggs cook to your liking.
8. Once the eggs are set, sprinkle with fresh parsley.
9. Serve hot with crusty bread.

HULU MUR (SUDANESE SWEET PORRIDGE)

- **Servings:** 4
- **Time:** 25 minutes

Ingredients:

- 1 cup millet or sorghum flour
- 4 cups water
- 1 cup coconut milk
- 1/2 cup sugar (adjust to taste)
- 1/4 teaspoon ground cinnamon
- 1/4 teaspoon ground cardamom

- Pinch of salt
- Nuts or raisins for garnish (optional)

Instructions:

1. In a bowl, mix millet or sorghum flour with water to make a smooth paste.
2. Pour the mixture into a pot and add coconut milk.
3. Cook over medium heat, stirring continuously to avoid lumps.
4. Add sugar, ground cinnamon, ground cardamom, and a pinch of salt.
5. Continue stirring and cooking until the porridge thickens.
6. Taste and adjust sweetness if needed.
7. Once the desired consistency is reached, remove from heat.
8. Allow to cool slightly before serving.
9. Garnish with nuts or raisins if desired.

BUREM (SUDANESE PANCAKES)

- **Servings:** 6
- **Time:** 30 minutes

Ingredients:

- 1 cup all-purpose flour
- 1 cup milk
- 1 egg
- 2 tablespoons sugar
- 1/2 teaspoon baking powder
- Pinch of salt

- Butter or oil for cooking

Instructions:

1. In a bowl, whisk together flour, sugar, baking powder, and a pinch of salt.
2. In a separate bowl, beat the egg and add milk.
3. Gradually add the wet ingredients to the dry ingredients, mixing until smooth.
4. Heat a non-stick pan over medium heat and add a bit of butter or oil.
5. Pour a ladle of batter onto the pan to form a pancake.
6. Cook until bubbles form on the surface, then flip and cook the other side until golden.
7. Repeat with the remaining batter.
8. Serve warm with your favorite toppings.

SOUPS AND STEWS

OKRA STEW

- **Servings:** 4
- **Time:** 40 minutes

Ingredients:

- 2 cups fresh okra, sliced
- 1 onion, finely chopped
- 2 tomatoes, diced
- 2 cloves garlic, minced
- 1 cup cooked chicken, shredded (optional)
- 2 tablespoons vegetable oil
- 1 teaspoon ground coriander
- 1 teaspoon ground cumin
- Salt and pepper to taste

- Fresh cilantro for garnish

Instructions:

1. In a pan, heat vegetable oil over medium heat.
2. Add chopped onions and sauté until translucent.
3. Stir in minced garlic and cook until fragrant.
4. Add diced tomatoes and cook until they break down.
5. Add sliced okra, shredded chicken (if using), ground coriander, ground cumin, salt, and pepper.
6. Cook for 20-25 minutes, stirring occasionally.
7. Adjust seasoning to taste.
8. Garnish with fresh cilantro before serving.

BAMIA (LAMB AND OKRA STEW)

- **Servings:** 6
- **Time:** 1 hour 30 minutes

Ingredients:

- 1.5 lbs lamb, cut into chunks
- 2 cups fresh okra, sliced
- 1 onion, finely chopped
- 3 tomatoes, diced
- 3 cloves garlic, minced
- 2 tablespoons tomato paste
- 3 tablespoons vegetable oil
- 1 teaspoon ground coriander
- 1 teaspoon ground cumin
- 1 teaspoon paprika
- Salt and pepper to taste
- Fresh parsley for garnish

Instructions:

1. In a pot, heat vegetable oil over medium heat.
2. Add chopped onions and sauté until golden.
3. Add minced garlic and cook until fragrant.
4. Add lamb chunks and brown on all sides.
5. Stir in diced tomatoes, tomato paste, ground coriander, ground cumin, paprika, salt, and pepper.
6. Add enough water to cover the meat, then cover the pot and simmer for 1 hour.
7. Add sliced okra to the pot and cook for an additional 20-30 minutes until tender.
8. Adjust seasoning to taste.
9. Garnish with fresh parsley before serving.

SHORBA (LENTIL SOUP)

- **Servings:** 4
- **Time:** 40 minutes

Ingredients:

- 1 cup red lentils, rinsed
- 1 onion, finely chopped
- 2 carrots, diced
- 2 tomatoes, chopped
- 3 cloves garlic, minced
- 1 teaspoon ground cumin
- 1 teaspoon ground coriander
- 1/2 teaspoon turmeric
- 6 cups vegetable or chicken broth
- 2 tablespoons olive oil
- Salt and pepper to taste

- Fresh parsley for garnish

Instructions:

1. In a pot, heat olive oil over medium heat.
2. Add chopped onions and sauté until softened.
3. Stir in minced garlic and cook until fragrant.
4. Add diced carrots and chopped tomatoes. Cook for 5 minutes.
5. Add rinsed red lentils, ground cumin, ground coriander, turmeric, salt, and pepper. Mix well.
6. Pour in the vegetable or chicken broth and bring to a boil.
7. Reduce heat, cover the pot, and simmer for 25-30 minutes until lentils are tender.
8. Use an immersion blender to partially blend the soup for a smoother texture (optional).
9. Adjust seasoning to taste.
10. Garnish with fresh parsley before serving.

MOLOKHIA SOUP (JUTE LEAF SOUP)

- **Servings:** 6
- **Time:** 1 hour

Ingredients:

- 2 cups fresh molokhia leaves, chopped (or frozen)
- 1 lb chicken, cut into pieces
- 1 onion, finely chopped
- 3 cloves garlic, minced
- 2 tomatoes, diced
- 2 tablespoons olive oil
- 1 teaspoon ground coriander

- 1 teaspoon ground cumin
- 1/2 teaspoon paprika
- 6 cups chicken broth
- Salt and pepper to taste
- Lemon wedges for serving

Instructions:

1. In a pot, heat olive oil over medium heat.
2. Add chopped onions and sauté until translucent.
3. Stir in minced garlic and cook until fragrant.
4. Add chicken pieces and brown on all sides.
5. Mix in diced tomatoes, ground coriander, ground cumin, paprika, salt, and pepper.
6. Pour in the chicken broth and bring to a boil.
7. Add chopped molokhia leaves to the pot and simmer for 30-40 minutes until chicken is cooked through.
8. Adjust seasoning to taste.
9. Serve hot with lemon wedges on the side.

ABEKHAW (SUDANESE LENTIL STEW)

- **Servings:** 4
- **Time:** 45 minutes

Ingredients:

- 1 cup brown lentils, rinsed
- 1 onion, finely chopped
- 2 tomatoes, diced
- 3 cloves garlic, minced
- 2 carrots, diced
- 2 tablespoons tomato paste

- 2 tablespoons vegetable oil
- 1 teaspoon ground cumin
- 1 teaspoon ground coriander
- 1/2 teaspoon paprika
- 4 cups vegetable broth
- Salt and pepper to taste
- Fresh cilantro for garnish

Instructions:

1. In a pot, heat vegetable oil over medium heat.
2. Add chopped onions and sauté until golden.
3. Stir in minced garlic and cook until fragrant.
4. Mix in diced tomatoes, tomato paste, ground cumin, ground coriander, and paprika. Cook for 5 minutes.
5. Add rinsed lentils and diced carrots to the pot.
6. Pour in vegetable broth and bring to a boil.
7. Reduce heat, cover the pot, and simmer for 30-35 minutes until lentils are tender.
8. Adjust seasoning with salt and pepper.
9. Garnish with fresh cilantro before serving.

BASSAS (MEAT AND VEGETABLE STEW)

- **Servings:** 6
- **Time:** 1 hour 30 minutes

Ingredients:

- 1.5 lbs lamb or beef, cut into chunks
- 2 onions, finely chopped
- 4 cloves garlic, minced
- 3 tomatoes, diced

- 2 carrots, diced
- 2 potatoes, peeled and diced
- 1 zucchini, diced
- 1 cup green beans, chopped
- 3 tablespoons tomato paste
- 3 tablespoons vegetable oil
- 1 teaspoon ground cumin
- 1 teaspoon ground coriander
- 1/2 teaspoon paprika
- Salt and pepper to taste
- Fresh parsley for garnish

Instructions:

1. In a pot, heat vegetable oil over medium heat.
2. Add chopped onions and sauté until translucent.
3. Stir in minced garlic and cook until fragrant.
4. Add meat chunks and brown on all sides.
5. Mix in diced tomatoes, tomato paste, ground cumin, ground coriander, paprika, salt, and pepper. Cook for 5 minutes.
6. Add diced carrots, potatoes, zucchini, and green beans to the pot.
7. Pour in enough water to cover the ingredients and bring to a boil.
8. Reduce heat, cover the pot, and simmer for 1 hour until meat and vegetables are tender.
9. Adjust seasoning to taste.
10. Garnish with fresh parsley before serving.

SHARMOOF (SUDANESE TRIPE STEW)

- **Servings:** 4

- **Time:** 2 hours

Ingredients:

- 1 lb beef tripe, cleaned and sliced
- 1 onion, finely chopped
- 4 cloves garlic, minced
- 2 tomatoes, diced
- 2 tablespoons tomato paste
- 3 tablespoons vegetable oil
- 1 teaspoon ground cumin
- 1 teaspoon ground coriander
- 1/2 teaspoon paprika
- 1/2 teaspoon ground turmeric
- Salt and pepper to taste
- Fresh cilantro for garnish
- Lemon wedges for serving

Instructions:

1. In a pot, heat vegetable oil over medium heat.
2. Add chopped onions and sauté until golden.
3. Stir in minced garlic and cook until fragrant.
4. Add sliced tripe and brown on all sides.
5. Mix in diced tomatoes, tomato paste, ground cumin, ground coriander, paprika, turmeric, salt, and pepper. Cook for 5 minutes.
6. Pour in enough water to cover the tripe and bring to a boil.
7. Reduce heat, cover the pot, and simmer for 1.5 to 2 hours until the tripe is tender.
8. Adjust seasoning to taste.
9. Garnish with fresh cilantro before serving.

10. Serve hot with lemon wedges on the side.

SALATA ASWAD (BLACK-EYED PEA STEW)

- **Servings:** 4
- **Time:** 1 hour

Ingredients:

- 2 cups dried black-eyed peas, soaked overnight
- 1 onion, finely chopped
- 3 tomatoes, diced
- 3 cloves garlic, minced
- 2 tablespoons tomato paste
- 3 tablespoons vegetable oil
- 1 teaspoon ground cumin
- 1 teaspoon ground coriander
- 1/2 teaspoon paprika
- 1/2 teaspoon ground turmeric
- Salt and pepper to taste
- Fresh parsley for garnish

Instructions:

1. In a pot, heat vegetable oil over medium heat.
2. Add chopped onions and sauté until translucent.
3. Stir in minced garlic and cook until fragrant.
4. Add soaked black-eyed peas and brown for a few minutes.
5. Mix in diced tomatoes, tomato paste, ground cumin, ground coriander, paprika, turmeric, salt, and pepper. Cook for 5 minutes.

6. Pour in enough water to cover the black-eyed peas and bring to a boil.
7. Reduce heat, cover the pot, and simmer for 45-60 minutes until the peas are tender.
8. Adjust seasoning to taste.
9. Garnish with fresh parsley before serving.

YALABOUR (CHICKEN AND PEANUT STEW)

- **Servings:** 4
- **Time:** 1 hour

Ingredients:

- 1 whole chicken, cut into pieces
- 1 cup peanuts, ground into a paste
- 1 onion, finely chopped
- 2 tomatoes, diced
- 3 cloves garlic, minced
- 2 tablespoons vegetable oil
- 2 tablespoons tomato paste
- 1 teaspoon ground cumin
- 1 teaspoon ground coriander
- 1/2 teaspoon paprika
- 1/2 teaspoon ground turmeric
- Salt and pepper to taste
- Fresh cilantro for garnish

Instructions:

1. In a pot, heat vegetable oil over medium heat.
2. Add chopped onions and sauté until golden.

3. Stir in minced garlic and cook until fragrant.
4. Add chicken pieces and brown on all sides.
5. Mix in diced tomatoes, tomato paste, ground cumin, ground coriander, paprika, turmeric, salt, and pepper. Cook for 5 minutes.
6. Pour in enough water to cover the chicken and bring to a boil.
7. Reduce heat, cover the pot, and simmer for 45-60 minutes until the chicken is cooked through.
8. Stir in the ground peanut paste and cook for an additional 15-20 minutes.
9. Adjust seasoning to taste.
10. Garnish with fresh cilantro before serving.

MARAQ (SUDANESE VEGETABLE SOUP)

- **Servings:** 6
- **Time:** 45 minutes

Ingredients:

- 1 onion, finely chopped
- 3 tomatoes, diced
- 3 carrots, diced
- 2 potatoes, peeled and diced
- 1 zucchini, diced
- 1 cup green beans, chopped
- 3 cloves garlic, minced
- 3 tablespoons tomato paste
- 3 tablespoons vegetable oil
- 1 teaspoon ground cumin
- 1 teaspoon ground coriander
- 1/2 teaspoon paprika

- 1/2 teaspoon ground turmeric
- 8 cups vegetable or chicken broth
- Salt and pepper to taste
- Fresh parsley for garnish

Instructions:

1. In a pot, heat vegetable oil over medium heat.
2. Add chopped onions and sauté until translucent.
3. Stir in minced garlic and cook until fragrant.
4. Mix in diced tomatoes, tomato paste, ground cumin, ground coriander, paprika, turmeric, salt, and pepper. Cook for 5 minutes.
5. Add diced carrots, potatoes, zucchini, and green beans to the pot.
6. Pour in vegetable or chicken broth and bring to a boil.
7. Reduce heat, cover the pot, and simmer for 30-40 minutes until the vegetables are tender.
8. Adjust seasoning to taste.
9. Garnish with fresh parsley before serving.

RICE AND GRAINS

MULAH SALAD (LENTIL AND RICE SALAD)

- **Servings:** 4
- **Time:** 45 minutes

Ingredients:

- 1 cup brown lentils, cooked
- 1 cup cooked basmati rice
- 1 red bell pepper, diced
- 1 cucumber, diced
- 1 red onion, finely chopped
- 1/4 cup fresh parsley, chopped
- 3 tablespoons olive oil
- 2 tablespoons lemon juice

- 1 teaspoon ground cumin
- Salt and pepper to taste
- Feta cheese for garnish (optional)

Instructions:

1. In a large bowl, combine cooked brown lentils, cooked basmati rice, diced red bell pepper, diced cucumber, chopped red onion, and chopped fresh parsley.
2. In a small bowl, whisk together olive oil, lemon juice, ground cumin, salt, and pepper to create the dressing.
3. Pour the dressing over the salad and toss to combine.
4. Garnish with crumbled feta cheese if desired.

MAHSHI (STUFFED GRAPE LEAVES)

- **Servings:** 6-8
- **Time:** 1 hour 30 minutes

Ingredients:

- 1 cup grape leaves, preserved in brine, rinsed
- 1 cup short-grain rice, uncooked
- 1/2 lb ground beef or lamb
- 1 onion, finely chopped
- 2 tomatoes, diced
- 2 tablespoons tomato paste
- 1/4 cup pine nuts
- 1/4 cup currants or raisins
- 1 teaspoon ground cinnamon
- 1 teaspoon ground allspice
- 1/2 teaspoon ground cumin
- Salt and pepper to taste

- 2 cups vegetable or chicken broth
- 3 tablespoons olive oil
- Lemon wedges for serving

Instructions:

1. Rinse the grape leaves under cold water and drain.
2. In a bowl, mix together uncooked rice, ground beef or lamb, chopped onion, diced tomatoes, tomato paste, pine nuts, currants or raisins, ground cinnamon, ground allspice, ground cumin, salt, and pepper.
3. Place a grape leaf flat on a surface, shiny side down, and add a spoonful of the rice mixture in the center.
4. Fold the sides of the grape leaf over the filling, then roll tightly from the bottom to form a small roll.
5. Repeat until all grape leaves are stuffed.
6. In a pot, arrange the stuffed grape leaves snugly.
7. Pour vegetable or chicken broth and olive oil over the stuffed grape leaves.
8. Place a heavy plate on top to prevent them from unraveling during cooking.
9. Simmer over low heat for 45-60 minutes until the rice is cooked and the grape leaves are tender.
10. Serve warm or at room temperature with lemon wedges on the side.

KOFTA BIRYANI

- **Servings:** 4-6
- **Time:** 1 hour 30 minutes

Ingredients:

For Kofta:

- 1 lb ground lamb or beef
- 1 onion, finely chopped
- 2 cloves garlic, minced
- 1/4 cup chopped fresh cilantro
- 1 teaspoon ground cumin
- 1 teaspoon ground coriander
- 1/2 teaspoon chili powder
- Salt and pepper to taste
- Vegetable oil for frying

For Rice:

- 2 cups basmati rice, soaked and drained
- 4 cups water
- 1 onion, thinly sliced
- 2 tomatoes, diced
- 1/4 cup plain yogurt
- 1/2 teaspoon turmeric powder
- 1/2 teaspoon chili powder
- 1/2 teaspoon ground cumin
- 1/2 teaspoon ground coriander
- Salt to taste

For Assembly:

- Fresh cilantro and mint for garnish
- Fried onions for topping (optional)

Instructions:

1. **Prepare Kofta:**

- o In a bowl, combine ground lamb or beef, chopped onion, minced garlic, chopped cilantro, ground cumin, ground coriander, chili powder, salt, and pepper.
- o Shape the mixture into small balls or cylinders to form koftas.
- o Heat vegetable oil in a pan and fry the koftas until browned. Set aside.

2. **Prepare Rice:**
   - o In a pot, heat a little vegetable oil and sauté the thinly sliced onion until golden brown.
   - o Add diced tomatoes and cook until they soften.
   - o Stir in plain yogurt, turmeric powder, chili powder, ground cumin, ground coriander, and salt.
   - o Add soaked and drained basmati rice to the pot and cook for a few minutes, coating the rice with the spices.
   - o Pour in water, bring to a boil, then reduce heat and simmer until the rice is almost cooked.

3. **Assembly:**
   - o In a deep ovenproof dish, layer half of the partially cooked rice.
   - o Arrange the fried koftas over the rice.
   - o Cover the koftas with the remaining rice.
   - o Garnish with fresh cilantro and mint.
   - o Optionally, top with fried onions for added flavor.
   - o Cover the dish tightly with foil and bake in a preheated oven at 350°F (175°C) for 20-25 minutes.

4. **Serve:**
   - o Gently fluff the rice with a fork.
- o Serve hot, ensuring each plate has a portion of koftas and flavorful rice.

KARKADEH RICE (HIBISCUS RICE)

- **Servings:** 4-6
- **Time:** 40 minutes

Ingredients:

- 2 cups basmati rice, washed and drained
- 4 cups water
- 1/2 cup dried hibiscus petals (karkadeh)
- 1 onion, finely chopped
- 2 tablespoons vegetable oil
- 1 teaspoon ground cumin
- 1 teaspoon ground coriander
- 1/2 teaspoon cinnamon
- Salt to taste
- Chopped fresh parsley for garnish

Instructions:

1. In a pot, heat vegetable oil over medium heat. Add chopped onions and sauté until translucent.
2. Stir in dried hibiscus petals and cook for a couple of minutes until they release their vibrant color.
3. Add washed and drained basmati rice to the pot. Stir to coat the rice with the hibiscus and onion mixture.
4. Pour in water, and add ground cumin, ground coriander, cinnamon, and salt. Stir to combine.
5. Bring the mixture to a boil, then reduce heat to low, cover the pot, and simmer for 15-20 minutes or until the rice is tender and the liquid is absorbed.
6. Once cooked, fluff the rice with a fork to separate the grains.

7. Garnish with chopped fresh parsley before serving.

ASEEDAH BIL DAMA (SORGHUM WITH OKRA)

- **Servings:** 4
- **Time:** 1 hour

Ingredients:

For Sorghum Base:

- 1 cup sorghum, soaked overnight
- 4 cups water
- Salt to taste

For Okra Stew:

- 1 cup fresh okra, sliced
- 1 onion, finely chopped
- 2 tomatoes, diced
- 3 cloves garlic, minced
- 2 tablespoons tomato paste
- 2 tablespoons vegetable oil
- 1 teaspoon ground coriander
- 1 teaspoon ground cumin
- 1/2 teaspoon paprika
- Salt and pepper to taste

Instructions:

1. **Prepare Sorghum Base:**

o Rinse soaked sorghum and place it in a pot with water.

o Bring to a boil, then reduce heat to low, cover, and simmer for 40-45 minutes or until sorghum is tender.

o Add salt to taste.

2. **Prepare Okra Stew:**

o In a separate pan, heat vegetable oil over medium heat.

o Add chopped onions and sauté until translucent.

o Stir in minced garlic and cook until fragrant.

o Add diced tomatoes, tomato paste, ground coriander, ground cumin, paprika, salt, and pepper. Cook for 5 minutes.

o Add sliced okra to the pan and cook for an additional 15-20 minutes until okra is tender.

3. **Serve:**

o Spoon a generous portion of the cooked sorghum onto a plate.

o Top the sorghum with the okra stew.

4. **Optional Garnish:**

o Garnish with fresh herbs like parsley or cilantro for added freshness.

BAMIA RICE (OKRA AND RICE)

- **Servings:** 4-6
- **Time:** 45 minutes

Ingredients:

- 2 cups basmati rice, washed and drained
- 4 cups water
- 1 lb fresh okra, sliced

- 1 onion, finely chopped
- 2 tomatoes, diced
- 3 cloves garlic, minced
- 2 tablespoons tomato paste
- 3 tablespoons vegetable oil
- 1 teaspoon ground coriander
- 1 teaspoon ground cumin
- 1/2 teaspoon paprika
- Salt and pepper to taste
- Fresh cilantro for garnish

Instructions:

1. In a pot, heat vegetable oil over medium heat. Add chopped onions and sauté until translucent.
2. Stir in minced garlic and cook until fragrant.
3. Add diced tomatoes, tomato paste, ground coriander, ground cumin, paprika, salt, and pepper. Cook for 5 minutes.
4. Add sliced okra to the pot and cook for an additional 15-20 minutes until okra is tender.
5. In a separate pot, bring 4 cups of water to a boil. Add washed and drained basmati rice. Cook until the rice is almost tender. Drain any excess water.
6. Mix the partially cooked rice with the okra mixture in the pot. Ensure the rice is evenly distributed.
7. Cover the pot and let it simmer on low heat for an additional 15-20 minutes until the rice is fully cooked.
8. Garnish with fresh cilantro before serving.

KESRA BEL DAMA (SORGHUM WITH TOMATOES)

- **Servings:** 4
- **Time:** 1 hour

Ingredients:

- 1 cup sorghum, soaked overnight
- 4 cups water
- 4 tomatoes, diced
- 1 onion, finely chopped
- 3 cloves garlic, minced
- 2 tablespoons tomato paste
- 3 tablespoons vegetable oil
- 1 teaspoon ground coriander
- 1 teaspoon ground cumin
- 1/2 teaspoon paprika
- Salt and pepper to taste
- Fresh parsley for garnish

Instructions:

1. Rinse soaked sorghum and place it in a pot with 4 cups of water.
2. Bring to a boil, then reduce heat to low, cover, and simmer for 40-45 minutes or until sorghum is tender. Add salt to taste.
3. In a separate pan, heat vegetable oil over medium heat.
4. Add chopped onions and sauté until translucent.
5. Stir in minced garlic and cook until fragrant.
6. Add diced tomatoes, tomato paste, ground coriander, ground cumin, paprika, salt, and pepper. Cook for 10-15 minutes until the tomatoes break down and the mixture thickens.

7. Combine the tomato mixture with the cooked sorghum and let it simmer for an additional 10 minutes, allowing the flavors to meld.
8. Garnish with fresh parsley before serving.

HASH (SUDANESE RICE WITH LENTILS)

- **Servings:** 4-6
- **Time:** 45 minutes

Ingredients:

- 2 cups basmati rice, washed and drained
- 1 cup brown lentils, rinsed
- 4 cups water
- 1 onion, finely chopped
- 2 tomatoes, diced
- 3 cloves garlic, minced
- 3 tablespoons vegetable oil
- 1 teaspoon ground cumin
- 1 teaspoon ground coriander
- 1/2 teaspoon paprika
- Salt and pepper to taste
- Fresh cilantro for garnish

Instructions:

1. In a pot, heat vegetable oil over medium heat. Add chopped onions and sauté until translucent.
2. Stir in minced garlic and cook until fragrant.
3. Add diced tomatoes, ground cumin, ground coriander, paprika, salt, and pepper. Cook for 5-7 minutes until the tomatoes soften.

4. Add brown lentils to the pot and mix well.
5. Pour in 4 cups of water and bring to a boil.
6. Add washed and drained basmati rice to the pot. Stir gently.
7. Reduce heat to low, cover the pot, and simmer for 20-25 minutes or until the rice and lentils are cooked and the liquid is absorbed.
8. Fluff the rice with a fork to separate the grains.
9. Garnish with fresh cilantro before serving.

KISRA BIL LAHMA (MEAT WITH SUDANESE FLATBREAD)

- **Servings:** 4-6
- **Time:** 1 hour

Ingredients:

For Sudanese Flatbread (Kisra):

- 2 cups sorghum flour
- 1 cup water
- Pinch of salt

For Meat Stew:

- 1 lb lamb or beef, cubed
- 1 onion, finely chopped
- 3 tomatoes, diced
- 3 cloves garlic, minced
- 3 tablespoons vegetable oil
- 2 tablespoons tomato paste
- 1 teaspoon ground coriander

- 1 teaspoon ground cumin
- 1/2 teaspoon paprika
- Salt and pepper to taste
- Fresh parsley for garnish

Instructions:

1. **Prepare Sudanese Flatbread (Kisra):**
   - In a bowl, mix sorghum flour, water, and a pinch of salt to form a thin batter.
   - Heat a non-stick pan over medium heat.
   - Pour a ladle of the batter onto the pan, spreading it thinly to create a flatbread.
   - Cook until the edges lift, then flip and cook the other side. Repeat until all the batter is used.
2. **Prepare Meat Stew:**
   - In a pot, heat vegetable oil over medium heat.
   - Add chopped onions and sauté until translucent.
   - Stir in minced garlic and cook until fragrant.
   - Add cubed lamb or beef and brown on all sides.
   - Mix in diced tomatoes, tomato paste, ground coriander, ground cumin, paprika, salt, and pepper. Cook for 10-15 minutes until the tomatoes break down and the mixture thickens.
   - Adjust seasoning to taste.
3. **Serve:**
   - Arrange pieces of Kisra on a plate.
   - Spoon the meat stew over the flatbread.
   - Garnish with fresh parsley before serving.

SHORBA ADDAS (RED LENTIL SOUP WITH RICE)

- **Servings:** 4-6
- **Time:** 45 minutes

Ingredients:

- 1 cup red lentils, rinsed
- 1/2 cup rice, washed and drained
- 1 onion, finely chopped
- 2 tomatoes, diced
- 3 cloves garlic, minced
- 3 tablespoons vegetable oil
- 2 tablespoons tomato paste
- 1 teaspoon ground cumin
- 1 teaspoon ground coriander
- 1/2 teaspoon paprika
- 8 cups vegetable or chicken broth
- Salt and pepper to taste
- Fresh cilantro for garnish

Instructions:

1. In a pot, heat vegetable oil over medium heat. Add chopped onions and sauté until translucent.
2. Stir in minced garlic and cook until fragrant.
3. Mix in diced tomatoes, tomato paste, ground cumin, ground coriander, paprika, salt, and pepper. Cook for 5-7 minutes until the tomatoes soften.
4. Add red lentils and rice to the pot. Stir well to coat them with the tomato mixture.
5. Pour in vegetable or chicken broth and bring to a boil.
6. Reduce heat, cover the pot, and simmer for 30-35 minutes until the lentils and rice are tender.
7. Adjust seasoning to taste.

8. Garnish with fresh cilantro before serving.

MEATY DELICACIES

MULUKHIYAH WITH MEAT

- **Servings:** 4-6
- **Time:** 1 hour

Ingredients:

- 2 cups fresh or frozen mulukhiyah leaves
- 1 lb chicken or beef, cut into pieces
- 1 onion, finely chopped
- 3 tomatoes, diced
- 3 cloves garlic, minced
- 3 tablespoons vegetable oil
- 2 tablespoons ground coriander
- 1 tablespoon ground cumin
- 1 teaspoon paprika

- Salt and pepper to taste
- 6 cups chicken or beef broth
- Juice of 1 lemon for serving
- Cooked rice for serving

Instructions:

1. In a pot, heat vegetable oil over medium heat. Add chopped onions and sauté until translucent.
2. Stir in minced garlic and cook until fragrant.
3. Add chicken or beef pieces and brown on all sides.
4. Mix in diced tomatoes, ground coriander, ground cumin, paprika, salt, and pepper. Cook for 10 minutes until the tomatoes break down.
5. Add mulukhiyah leaves to the pot and stir well.
6. Pour in chicken or beef broth and bring to a boil. Reduce heat, cover the pot, and simmer for 30-40 minutes until the meat is tender and the mulukhiyah is cooked.
7. Adjust seasoning to taste.
8. Serve hot over cooked rice, with a squeeze of lemon on top.

SAMAK TIBS (FISH TIBS)

- **Servings:** 4
- **Time:** 30 minutes

Ingredients:

- 1 lb firm white fish fillets, cut into chunks
- 1 onion, thinly sliced
- 2 tomatoes, diced
- 3 cloves garlic, minced

- 3 tablespoons olive oil
- 1 teaspoon ground cumin
- 1 teaspoon paprika
- 1/2 teaspoon chili powder
- Salt and pepper to taste
- Fresh cilantro for garnish
- Lemon wedges for serving

Instructions:

1. In a pan, heat olive oil over medium heat. Add thinly sliced onions and sauté until golden brown.
2. Stir in minced garlic and cook until fragrant.
3. Add fish chunks to the pan and cook until they are no longer translucent, flipping them gently to ensure even cooking.
4. Mix in diced tomatoes, ground cumin, paprika, chili powder, salt, and pepper. Cook for 5-7 minutes until the tomatoes soften and form a sauce.
5. Adjust seasoning to taste.
6. Garnish with fresh cilantro before serving.
7. Serve hot with lemon wedges on the side.

SUMAC CHICKEN

- **Servings:** 4
- **Time:** 1 hour

Ingredients:

- 4 chicken breasts, boneless and skinless
- 1/4 cup olive oil
- 2 tablespoons sumac

- 1 teaspoon ground cumin
- 1 teaspoon paprika
- 1 teaspoon garlic powder
- Salt and pepper to taste
- 1 lemon, sliced
- Fresh parsley for garnish

Instructions:

1. Preheat the oven to 375°F (190°C).
2. In a bowl, mix olive oil, sumac, ground cumin, paprika, garlic powder, salt, and pepper to create the marinade.
3. Place the chicken breasts in a dish and coat them evenly with the marinade. Allow them to marinate for at least 30 minutes.
4. Heat a skillet over medium-high heat. Sear the chicken breasts for 2-3 minutes on each side to achieve a golden brown color.
5. Transfer the chicken breasts to a baking dish. Arrange lemon slices on top.
6. Bake in the preheated oven for 25-30 minutes or until the chicken is cooked through.
7. Garnish with fresh parsley before serving.
8. Serve hot with your favorite side dishes.

KILICHI (DRIED MEAT)

- **Servings:** Varies
- **Time:** 1-2 days (including drying time)

Ingredients:

- 1 lb lean beef, thinly sliced

- 1 cup groundnut powder (ground peanuts)
- 1 tablespoon ground cayenne pepper
- 1 teaspoon garlic powder
- 1 teaspoon ginger powder
- 1 teaspoon onion powder
- Salt to taste

Instructions:

1. **Prepare the Meat:**
   - Trim excess fat from the beef and slice it thinly. It's crucial to use lean cuts for better drying.
2. **Marinate the Meat:**
   - In a bowl, combine groundnut powder, ground cayenne pepper, garlic powder, ginger powder, onion powder, and salt.
   - Rub the spice mixture onto each slice of meat, ensuring they are evenly coated.
   - Allow the meat to marinate for at least 4-6 hours, or preferably overnight in the refrigerator.
3. **Dry the Meat:**
   - Preheat your oven to the lowest setting or use a food dehydrator.
   - Place the marinated meat slices on a wire rack or directly on oven racks.
   - Dry the meat for 6-8 hours or until it reaches the desired level of dryness. You can also use a food dehydrator according to its instructions.
4. **Store Kilichi:**
   - Once dried, let the Kilichi cool completely.
   - Store in an airtight container in a cool, dry place.
5. **Serve:**

- o Kilichi can be enjoyed as a snack on its own or added to various dishes for extra flavor.

BEGRI (SUDANESE LAMB CURRY)

- **Servings:** 4-6
- **Time:** 1 hour 30 minutes

Ingredients:

- 2 lbs lamb, cut into cubes
- 2 onions, finely chopped
- 3 tomatoes, diced
- 3 cloves garlic, minced
- 2 tablespoons tomato paste
- 3 tablespoons vegetable oil
- 1 tablespoon ground coriander
- 1 tablespoon ground cumin
- 1 teaspoon ground turmeric
- 1/2 teaspoon chili powder (adjust to taste)
- Salt and pepper to taste
- 1 cup water
- Fresh cilantro for garnish

Instructions:

1. In a large pot, heat vegetable oil over medium heat. Add chopped onions and sauté until golden brown.
2. Stir in minced garlic and cook until fragrant.
3. Add lamb cubes to the pot and brown on all sides.
4. Mix in diced tomatoes, tomato paste, ground coriander, ground cumin, ground turmeric, chili powder, salt, and

pepper. Cook for 10-15 minutes until the tomatoes break down and the mixture thickens.

5. Pour in water and bring to a boil. Reduce heat, cover the pot, and simmer for 1 hour or until the lamb is tender.
6. Adjust seasoning to taste.
7. Garnish with fresh cilantro before serving.
8. Serve hot over rice or with Sudanese flatbread.

KEBDA ISKANDARANI (LIVER ISKANDERANI)

- **Servings:** 4-6
- **Time:** 45 minutes

Ingredients:

- 1 lb lamb or beef liver, sliced
- 1 onion, thinly sliced
- 2 tomatoes, diced
- 3 cloves garlic, minced
- 3 tablespoons vegetable oil
- 1 teaspoon ground cumin
- 1 teaspoon ground coriander
- 1/2 teaspoon chili powder (adjust to taste)
- Salt and pepper to taste
- Juice of 1 lemon
- Fresh parsley for garnish
- Pita bread or rice for serving

Instructions:

1. In a skillet, heat vegetable oil over medium heat. Add thinly sliced onions and sauté until golden brown.

2. Stir in minced garlic and cook until fragrant.
3. Add sliced liver to the skillet and cook until browned on the outside but still slightly pink inside.
4. Mix in diced tomatoes, ground cumin, ground coriander, chili powder, salt, and pepper. Cook for 5-7 minutes until the tomatoes soften.
5. Squeeze the lemon juice over the liver mixture and stir well.
6. Adjust seasoning to taste.
7. Garnish with fresh parsley before serving.
8. Serve hot with pita bread or over a bed of rice.

SAMAK MESHWI (GRILLED FISH)

- **Servings:** 4
- **Time:** 30 minutes

Ingredients:

- 4 whole fish (such as tilapia or sea bream), cleaned and gutted
- 1/4 cup olive oil
- Juice of 2 lemons
- 3 cloves garlic, minced
- 1 teaspoon ground cumin
- 1 teaspoon paprika
- 1/2 teaspoon cayenne pepper (adjust to taste)
- Salt and pepper to taste
- Fresh parsley for garnish
- Lemon wedges for serving

Instructions:

1. Preheat the grill to medium-high heat.
2. In a bowl, mix olive oil, lemon juice, minced garlic, ground cumin, paprika, cayenne pepper, salt, and pepper to create the marinade.
3. Score the fish on both sides with shallow cuts to help the marinade penetrate.
4. Brush the fish generously with the marinade, ensuring it gets into the cuts.
5. Place the fish on the preheated grill and cook for about 15-20 minutes, turning once, or until the fish is cooked through and has a nice char.
6. Baste the fish with the remaining marinade during grilling.
7. Garnish with fresh parsley.
8. Serve hot with lemon wedges on the side.

FASOULIA BEL LAHMA (MEAT AND BEAN STEW)

- **Servings:** 4-6
- **Time:** 1 hour 30 minutes

Ingredients:

- 1 lb lamb or beef, cubed
- 2 cups green beans, trimmed and cut into bite-sized pieces
- 1 onion, finely chopped
- 3 tomatoes, diced
- 3 cloves garlic, minced
- 3 tablespoons vegetable oil
- 2 tablespoons tomato paste

- 1 teaspoon ground cumin
- 1 teaspoon ground coriander
- 1/2 teaspoon paprika
- Salt and pepper to taste
- 2 cups water
- Fresh parsley for garnish

Instructions:

1. In a pot, heat vegetable oil over medium heat. Add chopped onions and sauté until translucent.
2. Stir in minced garlic and cook until fragrant.
3. Add cubed lamb or beef and brown on all sides.
4. Mix in diced tomatoes, tomato paste, ground cumin, ground coriander, paprika, salt, and pepper. Cook for 10-15 minutes until the tomatoes break down and the mixture thickens.
5. Add green beans to the pot and stir well.
6. Pour in water and bring to a boil. Reduce heat, cover the pot, and simmer for 1 hour or until the meat is tender and the beans are cooked.
7. Adjust seasoning to taste.
8. Garnish with fresh parsley before serving.
9. Serve hot with Sudanese flatbread or over rice.

TIBS FIRFIR (SPICY BEEF STEW)

- **Servings:** 4-6
- **Time:** 1 hour

Ingredients:

- 1 lb beef, thinly sliced

- 1 onion, finely chopped
- 2 tomatoes, diced
- 3 cloves garlic, minced
- 3 tablespoons vegetable oil
- 2 tablespoons berbere spice blend
- 1 teaspoon ground cumin
- 1 teaspoon ground coriander
- 1/2 teaspoon paprika
- Salt and pepper to taste
- 1 cup beef broth
- Injera (Ethiopian flatbread) or pita bread for serving

Instructions:

1. In a pan, heat vegetable oil over medium heat. Add chopped onions and sauté until golden brown.
2. Stir in minced garlic and cook until fragrant.
3. Add thinly sliced beef to the pan and cook until browned on all sides.
4. Mix in diced tomatoes, berbere spice blend, ground cumin, ground coriander, paprika, salt, and pepper. Cook for 10-15 minutes until the tomatoes break down and the mixture thickens.
5. Pour in beef broth and bring to a simmer. Allow it to cook for an additional 15-20 minutes until the beef is tender.
6. Adjust seasoning to taste.
7. Serve the Tibs Firfir hot over torn pieces of injera or with pita bread.

DUKKU (GROUNDNUT ROLL)

- **Servings:** 8-10

- **Time:** 1 hour (plus chilling time)

Ingredients:

For the Groundnut Paste:

- 2 cups roasted peanuts, finely ground
- 1 cup grated coconut
- 1 cup millet flour
- 1 cup water
- 1/2 cup honey or maple syrup (adjust to taste)
- 1 teaspoon ground ginger
- 1/2 teaspoon ground cloves
- 1/2 teaspoon ground cinnamon
- Pinch of salt

For the Dough:

- 2 cups millet flour
- 1 cup water
- Pinch of salt

Instructions:

1. **Prepare the Groundnut Paste:**
   - In a bowl, combine finely ground roasted peanuts, grated coconut, millet flour, water, honey or maple syrup, ground ginger, ground cloves, ground cinnamon, and a pinch of salt.
   - Mix well until a thick and smooth paste is formed.
2. **Prepare the Dough:**
   - In a separate bowl, mix millet flour, water, and a pinch of salt to form a soft dough.
3. **Assemble the Dukku:**

- o Take a portion of the dough and flatten it into a thin, round disc on a clean surface.
- o Spread a generous layer of the groundnut paste on the dough.
- o Roll the dough with the paste into a log shape, ensuring it is tightly sealed.
- o Repeat the process until all the dough and groundnut paste are used.

4. **Chill and Serve:**
   - o Wrap the rolled Dukku logs in plastic wrap and refrigerate for at least 2 hours to allow them to firm up.
- o Once chilled, slice the Dukku into rounds before serving.

VEGETARIAN WONDERS

SALATA KHADRA (GREEN SALAD)

- **Servings:** 4
- **Time:** 15 minutes

Ingredients:

- 4 cups mixed salad greens (lettuce, spinach, arugula)
- 1 cucumber, thinly sliced
- 2 tomatoes, diced
- 1 green bell pepper, sliced
- 1 red onion, thinly sliced
- 1/4 cup fresh mint leaves, chopped
- 2 tablespoons olive oil
- Juice of 1 lemon
- Salt and pepper to taste

Instructions:

1. Wash and dry the mixed salad greens, then place them in a large salad bowl.
2. Add thinly sliced cucumber, diced tomatoes, sliced green bell pepper, and thinly sliced red onion to the bowl.
3. Sprinkle chopped fresh mint leaves over the salad for a burst of flavor.
4. Drizzle olive oil and squeeze the juice of one lemon over the salad.
5. Season the salad with salt and pepper to taste. Toss all the ingredients together until well combined.
6. Transfer the green salad to a serving platter or individual plates.

KAMOUNIA (SUDANESE BEAN STEW)

- **Servings:** 4-6
- **Time:** 1 hour 30 minutes

Ingredients:

- 2 cups red kidney beans, soaked overnight
- 1 onion, finely chopped
- 3 tomatoes, diced
- 3 cloves garlic, minced
- 3 tablespoons vegetable oil
- 2 tablespoons tomato paste
- 1 teaspoon ground cumin
- 1 teaspoon ground coriander
- 1/2 teaspoon paprika
- 1/2 teaspoon ground cinnamon
- Salt and pepper to taste

- 4 cups vegetable or beef broth
- Fresh cilantro for garnish
- Cooked rice for serving

Instructions:

1. Rinse the soaked red kidney beans and set aside.
2. In a pot, heat vegetable oil over medium heat. Add chopped onions and sauté until translucent.
3. Stir in minced garlic and cook until fragrant.
4. Add diced tomatoes, tomato paste, ground cumin, ground coriander, paprika, ground cinnamon, salt, and pepper. Cook for 10-15 minutes until the tomatoes break down and the mixture thickens.
5. Add soaked red kidney beans to the pot and mix well.
6. Pour in vegetable or beef broth and bring to a boil. Reduce heat, cover the pot, and simmer for 1 hour or until the beans are tender.
7. Adjust seasoning to taste.
8. Garnish with fresh cilantro before serving.
9. Serve hot over cooked rice.

BAMIA BIL ZEIT (OKRA IN OLIVE OIL)

- **Servings:** 4-6
- **Time:** 45 minutes

Ingredients:

- 2 cups fresh okra, washed and trimmed
- 1 onion, finely chopped
- 3 tomatoes, diced
- 3 cloves garlic, minced

- 1/2 cup olive oil
- 1 teaspoon ground coriander
- 1 teaspoon ground cumin
- 1/2 teaspoon paprika
- Salt and pepper to taste
- Juice of 1 lemon
- Fresh parsley for garnish

Instructions:

1. Heat olive oil in a pan over medium heat. Add chopped onions and sauté until translucent.
2. Stir in minced garlic and cook until fragrant.
3. Add diced tomatoes to the pan and cook until they start to break down.
4. Mix in ground coriander, ground cumin, paprika, salt, and pepper. Stir well.
5. Add fresh okra to the pan and coat them with the tomato and spice mixture.
6. Cover the pan and let the okra cook for about 20-25 minutes, stirring occasionally, until they are tender.
7. Squeeze the lemon juice over the okra and mix gently.
8. Adjust seasoning to taste.
9. Garnish with fresh parsley before serving.

FASOLIA BEL ZEIT (GREEN BEAN SALAD)

- **Servings:** 4-6
- **Time:** 30 minutes

Ingredients:

- 2 cups green beans, trimmed and cut into bite-sized pieces
- 1 red onion, thinly sliced
- 2 tomatoes, diced
- 1/4 cup black olives, sliced
- 1/4 cup feta cheese, crumbled
- 3 tablespoons olive oil
- 1 tablespoon red wine vinegar
- 1 teaspoon dried oregano
- Salt and pepper to taste
- Fresh parsley for garnish

Instructions:

1. In a pot of boiling water, blanch the green beans for 2-3 minutes until they are bright green and slightly tender. Drain and transfer to a bowl of ice water to stop the cooking process. Drain again.
2. In a large salad bowl, combine blanched green beans, thinly sliced red onion, diced tomatoes, sliced black olives, and crumbled feta cheese.
3. In a small bowl, whisk together olive oil, red wine vinegar, dried oregano, salt, and pepper to create the dressing.
4. Pour the dressing over the salad and toss gently to coat all the ingredients.
5. Adjust salt and pepper to taste.
6. Garnish with fresh parsley before serving.

ABELONEH (STUFFED ZUCCHINI)

- **Servings:** 4-6
- **Time:** 1 hour

Ingredients:

For the Stuffed Zucchini:

- 6 medium-sized zucchini
- 1 cup cooked rice
- 1 cup cooked lentils
- 1 onion, finely chopped
- 3 tomatoes, diced
- 3 cloves garlic, minced
- 3 tablespoons olive oil
- 1 teaspoon ground cumin
- 1 teaspoon ground coriander
- 1/2 teaspoon paprika
- Salt and pepper to taste

For the Tomato Sauce:

- 1 can (14 oz) crushed tomatoes
- 1 teaspoon dried basil
- 1 teaspoon dried oregano
- Salt and pepper to taste

Instructions:

1. **Prepare the Zucchini:**
   - Cut each zucchini in half lengthwise. Scoop out the center using a spoon, leaving a boat-shaped shell. Reserve the scooped-out flesh.
2. **Prepare the Filling:**
   - In a pan, heat olive oil over medium heat. Add chopped onions and sauté until translucent.
   - Stir in minced garlic and cook until fragrant.

- o Add diced tomatoes and the reserved zucchini flesh. Cook for 5-7 minutes until the tomatoes break down.
- o Mix in cooked rice, cooked lentils, ground cumin, ground coriander, paprika, salt, and pepper. Cook for an additional 5 minutes.

3. **Stuff the Zucchini:**
   - o Fill each zucchini half with the prepared filling.
4. **Prepare the Tomato Sauce:**
   - o In a bowl, mix crushed tomatoes, dried basil, dried oregano, salt, and pepper to create the sauce.
5. **Bake:**
   - o Preheat the oven to 375°F (190°C).
   - o Place the stuffed zucchini in a baking dish. Pour the tomato sauce over the zucchini.
   - o Cover the dish with aluminum foil and bake for 30-40 minutes or until the zucchini is tender.
6. **Serve:**
   - o Serve the Abeloneh hot, garnished with fresh herbs if desired.

RENGA RENGA (SPINACH STEW)

- • **Servings:** 4-6
- • **Time:** 30 minutes

Ingredients:

- • 1 lb fresh spinach, washed and chopped
- • 1 onion, finely chopped
- • 3 tomatoes, diced
- • 3 cloves garlic, minced
- • 3 tablespoons vegetable oil
- • 1 teaspoon ground coriander

- 1 teaspoon ground cumin
- 1/2 teaspoon turmeric
- 1/2 teaspoon paprika
- Salt and pepper to taste
- 1 cup vegetable or chicken broth
- Juice of 1 lemon

Instructions:

1. In a pan, heat vegetable oil over medium heat. Add chopped onions and sauté until translucent.
2. Stir in minced garlic and cook until fragrant.
3. Add diced tomatoes to the pan and cook until they start to break down.
4. Mix in ground coriander, ground cumin, turmeric, paprika, salt, and pepper. Stir well.
5. Add chopped spinach to the pan and coat it with the tomato and spice mixture.
6. Pour in vegetable or chicken broth and bring to a simmer. Allow it to cook for about 15-20 minutes until the spinach is wilted and tender.
7. Squeeze the lemon juice over the stew and mix gently.
8. Adjust seasoning to taste.
9. Serve the Renga Renga hot, with Sudanese flatbread or over rice.

BAMIA BIL TOM (OKRA WITH TOMATOES)

- **Servings:** 4-6
- **Time:** 45 minutes

Ingredients:

- 2 cups fresh okra, washed and trimmed
- 1 onion, finely chopped
- 3 tomatoes, diced
- 3 cloves garlic, minced
- 3 tablespoons vegetable oil
- 1 teaspoon ground coriander
- 1 teaspoon ground cumin
- 1/2 teaspoon paprika
- Salt and pepper to taste
- 1 cup tomato sauce
- Fresh cilantro for garnish
- Cooked rice for serving

Instructions:

1. In a pan, heat vegetable oil over medium heat. Add chopped onions and sauté until translucent.
2. Stir in minced garlic and cook until fragrant.
3. Add diced tomatoes to the pan and cook until they start to break down.
4. Mix in ground coriander, ground cumin, paprika, salt, and pepper. Stir well.
5. Add fresh okra to the pan and coat it with the tomato and spice mixture.
6. Pour in tomato sauce and bring to a simmer. Allow it to cook for about 20-25 minutes until the okra is tender.
7. Adjust seasoning to taste.
8. Garnish with fresh cilantro before serving.
9. Serve the Bamia Bil Tom hot over cooked rice.

DOLMA (STUFFED VEGETABLES)

- **Servings:** 4-6

- **Time:** 1 hour 30 minutes

Ingredients:

For the Filling:

- 1 cup rice, washed and soaked
- 1/2 lb ground lamb or beef
- 1 onion, finely chopped
- 3 tomatoes, diced
- 3 cloves garlic, minced
- 1/4 cup pine nuts
- 1/4 cup raisins
- 2 tablespoons tomato paste
- 2 tablespoons olive oil
- 1 teaspoon ground cinnamon
- 1 teaspoon ground allspice
- Salt and pepper to taste

For the Vegetables:

- 6 large zucchini
- 6 large bell peppers (mix of colors)
- Grape leaves, if available
- 3 cups vegetable or chicken broth
- Juice of 1 lemon

Instructions:

1. **Prepare the Filling:**
   - In a bowl, combine soaked rice, ground lamb or beef, chopped onions, diced tomatoes, minced garlic, pine nuts, raisins, tomato paste, olive oil, ground

cinnamon, ground allspice, salt, and pepper. Mix well.

2. **Prepare the Vegetables:**
   o If using zucchini, cut them in half lengthwise and scoop out the centers to create a boat-like shape.
   o If using bell peppers, cut off the tops and remove the seeds.
   o If using grape leaves, blanch them in boiling water for a few minutes to soften.
3. **Stuff the Vegetables:**
   o Stuff each vegetable with the rice and meat mixture, pressing it down gently.
4. **Arrange in a Pot:**
   o In a pot, arrange the stuffed vegetables snugly.
5. **Cook:**
   o Pour vegetable or chicken broth over the stuffed vegetables.
   o Squeeze the lemon juice over the top.
   o Cover the pot and simmer on low heat for 1 hour or until the rice is cooked and the vegetables are tender.
6. **Serve:**
   o Serve the Dolma hot, garnished with fresh herbs if desired.

SALATAT JARJEER (ARUGULA SALAD)

- **Servings:** 4
- **Time:** 15 minutes

Ingredients:

- 4 cups arugula, washed and dried
- 1 cup cherry tomatoes, halved

- 1/4 cup red onion, thinly sliced
- 1/4 cup pine nuts, toasted
- 1/4 cup feta cheese, crumbled
- 2 tablespoons olive oil
- 1 tablespoon balsamic vinegar
- Salt and pepper to taste

Instructions:

1. In a large salad bowl, combine arugula, halved cherry tomatoes, thinly sliced red onion, toasted pine nuts, and crumbled feta cheese.
2. In a small bowl, whisk together olive oil, balsamic vinegar, salt, and pepper to create the dressing.
3. Pour the dressing over the salad and toss gently to coat all the ingredients.
4. Adjust salt and pepper to taste.

SUDANESE LENTIL SALAD

- **Servings:** 4
- **Time:** 30 minutes

Ingredients:

- 1 cup green or brown lentils, cooked and drained
- 1 cucumber, diced
- 2 tomatoes, diced
- 1 red onion, finely chopped
- 1/4 cup fresh parsley, chopped
- 1/4 cup olive oil
- Juice of 1 lemon
- 2 cloves garlic, minced

- 1 teaspoon ground cumin
- Salt and pepper to taste

Instructions:

1. In a large bowl, combine cooked lentils, diced cucumber, diced tomatoes, chopped red onion, and fresh parsley.
2. In a small bowl, whisk together olive oil, lemon juice, minced garlic, ground cumin, salt, and pepper to create the dressing.
3. Pour the dressing over the lentil mixture and toss gently to coat all the ingredients.
4. Adjust salt and pepper to taste.
5. Allow the salad to marinate for at least 15 minutes before serving.

SWEETS AND DESSERTS

BASBOUSA (SEMOLINA CAKE)

- **Servings:** 12
- **Time:** 1 hour

Ingredients:

For the Cake:

- 2 cups semolina
- 1 cup plain yogurt
- 1 cup granulated sugar
- 1 cup desiccated coconut
- 1/2 cup unsalted butter, melted
- 1 teaspoon baking powder
- 1/2 teaspoon baking soda

- 1 teaspoon vanilla extract
- 1/4 cup blanched almonds or pine nuts for garnish

For the Sugar Syrup:

- 1 cup granulated sugar
- 1/2 cup water
- Juice of 1/2 lemon

Instructions:

1. **Prepare the Cake:**
   - Preheat the oven to 350°F (175°C). Grease a baking pan with butter or cooking spray.
   - In a large bowl, mix together semolina, plain yogurt, granulated sugar, desiccated coconut, melted butter, baking powder, baking soda, and vanilla extract until well combined.
2. **Bake the Cake:**
   - Pour the batter into the prepared baking pan, smoothing the top with a spatula.
   - Bake in the preheated oven for 30-40 minutes or until the top is golden brown and a toothpick inserted into the center comes out clean.
3. **Prepare the Sugar Syrup:**
   - In a saucepan, combine granulated sugar, water, and lemon juice. Bring to a boil, then reduce the heat and simmer for 10 minutes or until the syrup slightly thickens.
4. **Syrup the Basbousa:**
   - Once the cake is done, remove it from the oven and immediately pour the prepared sugar syrup evenly over the hot cake.

- o Allow the Basbousa to absorb the syrup and cool for at least 30 minutes.
5. **Garnish and Serve:**
- o Decorate the Basbousa with blanched almonds or pine nuts.
- o Cut the cake into diamond or square-shaped pieces and serve.

GURASA (SUDANESE COCONUT BREAD)

- **Servings:** 8
- **Time:** 2 hours (including rising time)

Ingredients:

- 4 cups all-purpose flour
- 1 cup desiccated coconut
- 1/2 cup granulated sugar
- 1 tablespoon active dry yeast
- 1 teaspoon salt
- 1 cup warm water
- 1/2 cup coconut milk
- 1/4 cup vegetable oil
- 1 teaspoon vanilla extract
- Additional desiccated coconut for topping

Instructions:

1. **Activate the Yeast:**
- o In a small bowl, combine warm water, a pinch of sugar, and active dry yeast. Allow it to sit for 5-10 minutes until it becomes frothy.
2. **Prepare the Dough:**

- o In a large mixing bowl, combine flour, desiccated coconut, granulated sugar, and salt.
- o Add the activated yeast mixture, coconut milk, vegetable oil, and vanilla extract to the dry ingredients. Mix to form a dough.
- o Knead the dough on a floured surface for about 10 minutes until it becomes smooth and elastic.

3. **First Rise:**
   - o Place the dough in a greased bowl, cover it with a damp cloth, and let it rise in a warm place for 1 hour or until it doubles in size.

4. **Shape and Second Rise:**
   - o Punch down the risen dough and divide it into 8 equal portions.
   - o Shape each portion into a round ball and place them on a greased baking sheet.
   - o Cover the shaped dough balls with a damp cloth and let them rise for an additional 30 minutes.

5. **Bake the Gurasa:**
   - o Preheat the oven to 350°F (175°C).
   - o Brush the tops of the risen dough balls with a bit of coconut milk and sprinkle desiccated coconut over each.
   - o Bake in the preheated oven for 20-25 minutes or until the Gurasa turns golden brown.

6. **Cool and Serve:**
   - o Allow the Gurasa to cool on a wire rack.
- o Serve the Sudanese Coconut Bread as a delightful accompaniment to tea or enjoy it on its own.

ZALABIA (SWEET DUMPLINGS)

- **Servings:** 12-15
- **Time:** 2 hours (including resting time)

Ingredients:

For the Dough:

- 2 cups all-purpose flour
- 1 cup warm water
- 1 teaspoon active dry yeast
- 1/2 teaspoon sugar
- 1/4 teaspoon salt

For the Sugar Syrup:

- 1 cup granulated sugar
- 1/2 cup water
- 1 tablespoon lemon juice
- 1 teaspoon orange blossom water (optional)

For Frying:

- Vegetable oil for deep frying

Instructions:

1. **Activate the Yeast:**
   o In a small bowl, combine warm water, active dry yeast, and sugar. Allow it to sit for 5-10 minutes until it becomes frothy.
2. **Prepare the Dough:**
   o In a large mixing bowl, combine flour and salt. Add the activated yeast mixture and mix to form a smooth dough.

o Cover the bowl with a damp cloth and let the dough rest in a warm place for 1 hour or until it doubles in size.

3. **Shape the Dumplings:**
   o Heat vegetable oil in a deep fryer or a deep, heavy-bottomed pan to 350°F (175°C).
   o Dip your hands in water to prevent sticking, take a small portion of the dough, and shape it into a ball or a ring. Repeat with the remaining dough.

4. **Fry the Zalabia:**
   o Carefully drop the shaped dough into the hot oil and fry until golden brown, turning occasionally for even cooking.
   o Use a slotted spoon to remove the fried zalabia and place them on a paper towel to absorb excess oil.

5. **Prepare the Sugar Syrup:**
   o In a saucepan, combine granulated sugar, water, and lemon juice. Bring to a boil, then reduce the heat and simmer for 5-7 minutes until the syrup slightly thickens.
   o Add orange blossom water if using and stir.

6. **Soak the Zalabia:**
   o Dip each fried zalabia into the sugar syrup, ensuring they are well coated. Allow them to soak for a few seconds.

7. **Serve:**
   o Serve the sweet zalabia on a platter, drizzling any remaining sugar syrup over the top.

TAMRIYAH (DATE BARS)

- **Servings:** 12-15 bars

- **Time:** 1 hour

Ingredients:

For the Date Filling:

- 2 cups dates, pitted and chopped
- 1 cup water
- 1 tablespoon butter
- 1 teaspoon vanilla extract

For the Oat Crust:

- 1 cup rolled oats
- 1 cup all-purpose flour
- 1/2 cup brown sugar, packed
- 1/2 teaspoon baking soda
- 1/2 cup unsalted butter, melted
- 1/4 teaspoon salt

Instructions:

1. **Prepare the Date Filling:**
   o In a saucepan, combine chopped dates, water, and butter. Cook over medium heat, stirring frequently, until the dates soften and the mixture thickens.
   o Remove from heat, stir in vanilla extract, and set aside to cool.
2. **Preheat the Oven:**
   o Preheat your oven to 350°F (175°C). Grease a baking pan or line it with parchment paper.
3. **Prepare the Oat Crust:**

- o In a mixing bowl, combine rolled oats, all-purpose flour, brown sugar, baking soda, melted butter, and salt. Mix until the ingredients come together.
- o Press about two-thirds of the oat mixture into the bottom of the prepared baking pan to create the crust.

4. **Assemble the Bars:**
- o Spread the cooled date filling evenly over the oat crust.
- o Sprinkle the remaining oat mixture over the date filling, pressing it lightly.

5. **Bake:**
- o Bake in the preheated oven for 25-30 minutes or until the top is golden brown.

6. **Cool and Slice:**
- o Allow the Tamriyah to cool completely in the pan before slicing into bars.

7. **Serve:**
- o Serve the date bars as a delightful treat with a cup of tea or coffee.

HAREESEH (SESAME CANDY)

- **Servings:** Approximately 20 pieces
- **Time:** 30 minutes

Ingredients:

- 1 cup sesame seeds
- 1 cup tahini (sesame paste)
- 1 cup powdered sugar
- 1 teaspoon vanilla extract

Instructions:

1. **Toast Sesame Seeds:**
    o   In a dry skillet over medium heat, toast the sesame seeds until they are golden brown and fragrant. Stir continuously to prevent burning. Once toasted, set aside to cool.
2. **Prepare the Mixture:**
    o   In a mixing bowl, combine the toasted sesame seeds, tahini, powdered sugar, and vanilla extract. Mix until all the ingredients are well combined.
3. **Shape the Candy:**
    o   Take small portions of the mixture and shape them into small, bite-sized rounds or squares. You can also press the mixture into a small pan and cut it into squares later.
4. **Let it Set:**
    o   Allow the shaped sesame candy to set at room temperature for at least 15-20 minutes. This helps them hold their shape.
5. **Serve:**
    o   Once set, your Hareeseh sesame candy is ready to be served.

GURRAT EL EID (SUDANESE EID COOKIES)

*   **Servings:** Approximately 30 cookies
*   **Time:** 1 hour

Ingredients:

*   2 cups all-purpose flour
*   1 cup semolina

- 1 cup powdered sugar
- 1 cup unsalted butter, softened
- 1 teaspoon baking powder
- 1/4 cup sesame seeds (for coating)

Instructions:

1. **Preheat the Oven:**
   - Preheat your oven to 350°F (175°C). Line a baking sheet with parchment paper.
2. **Prepare the Dough:**
   - In a large mixing bowl, combine all-purpose flour, semolina, powdered sugar, softened butter, and baking powder. Knead the ingredients until you have a smooth dough.
3. **Shape the Cookies:**
   - Take small portions of the dough and shape them into small balls or crescents. You can experiment with different shapes if desired.
4. **Coat with Sesame Seeds:**
   - Roll each cookie in sesame seeds, ensuring they are well-coated. This gives the cookies a delightful crunch.
5. **Arrange on Baking Sheet:**
   - Place the shaped and coated cookies on the prepared baking sheet, leaving some space between each.
6. **Bake:**
   - Bake in the preheated oven for 12-15 minutes or until the cookies turn golden brown around the edges.
7. **Cool and Serve:**
   - Allow the Gurrat El Eid cookies to cool on the baking sheet for a few minutes before transferring them to a wire rack to cool completely.

MUDAFFARA (SUDANESE FRUIT SALAD)

- **Servings:** 4-6
- **Time:** 20 minutes

Ingredients:

- 2 oranges, peeled and segmented
- 1 cup pineapple chunks
- 1 cup watermelon, diced
- 1 cup cantaloupe, diced
- 1 cup grapes, halved
- 1 banana, sliced
- 1 tablespoon honey (optional)
- Fresh mint leaves for garnish

Instructions:

1. **Prepare the Fruits:**
   - Peel and segment the oranges.
   - Dice the watermelon and cantaloupe into bite-sized pieces.
   - Cut the pineapple into chunks.
   - Halve the grapes.
   - Slice the banana.
2. **Combine the Fruits:**
   - In a large mixing bowl, combine all the prepared fruits.
3. **Optional Sweetening:**
   - If desired, drizzle honey over the fruit salad and gently toss to coat. Adjust the sweetness to your liking.
4. **Chill:**

- o Place the fruit salad in the refrigerator for at least 15-20 minutes to allow the flavors to meld and the salad to chill.
5. **Garnish and Serve:**
   - o Before serving, garnish the Mudaffara with fresh mint leaves.
- o Serve the refreshing Sudanese fruit salad as a side dish, dessert, or a light and healthy snack.

ARADAIB (SUDANESE HONEYCOMB TOFFEE)

- **Servings:** Approximately 20 pieces
- **Time:** 30 minutes

Ingredients:

- 1 cup granulated sugar
- 1/4 cup water
- 3 tablespoons honey
- 1 tablespoon white vinegar
- 1 teaspoon baking soda
- 1 teaspoon vanilla extract
- Vegetable oil for greasing

Instructions:

1. **Prepare the Pan:**
   - o Grease a square or rectangular baking pan with vegetable oil. Set aside.
2. **Combine Ingredients:**

o In a medium-sized saucepan, combine granulated sugar, water, honey, and white vinegar. Stir over medium heat until the sugar dissolves.

3. **Cook the Syrup:**
   o Allow the syrup to come to a boil, then reduce the heat to medium-low and let it simmer without stirring until it reaches a light amber color. This may take about 10-15 minutes.

4. **Add Baking Soda:**
   o Remove the saucepan from heat and quickly stir in the baking soda. The mixture will bubble up and expand, forming a frothy texture.

5. **Add Vanilla Extract:**
   o Stir in the vanilla extract, ensuring it's well incorporated into the frothy mixture.

6. **Pour into the Pan:**
   o Immediately pour the hot mixture into the prepared baking pan. Do not spread it too much; let it settle naturally.

7. **Cool and Break:**
   o Allow the Aradaib to cool and harden at room temperature for at least 20-30 minutes.
   o Once cooled and set, break the honeycomb toffee into bite-sized pieces.

8. **Serve:**
   o Serve the Aradaib as a delightful sweet treat or use it as a crunchy topping for desserts.

MEASUREMENT CONVERSIONS

Volume Conversions:

- 1 cup = 8 fluid ounces = 240 milliliters
- 1 tablespoon = 3 teaspoons = 15 milliliters
- 1 fluid ounce = 2 tablespoons = 30 milliliters
- 1 quart = 4 cups = 32 fluid ounces = 946 milliliters
- 1 gallon = 4 quarts = 128 fluid ounces = 3.78 liters
- 1 liter = 1,000 milliliters = 33.8 fluid ounces
- 1 milliliter = 0.034 fluid ounces = 0.002 cups

Weight Conversions:

- 1 pound = 16 ounces = 453.592 grams
- 1 ounce = 28.349 grams
- 1 gram = 0.035 ounces = 0.001 kilograms
- 1 kilogram = 1,000 grams = 35.274 ounces = 2.205 pounds

Temperature Conversions:

- To convert from Fahrenheit to Celsius: (°F - 32) / 1.8
- To convert from Celsius to Fahrenheit: (°C * 1.8) + 32

Length Conversions:

- 1 inch = 2.54 centimeters
- 1 foot = 12 inches = 30.48 centimeters
- 1 yard = 3 feet = 36 inches = 91.44 centimeters
- 1 meter = 100 centimeters = 1.094 yards.

Printed in Great Britain
by Amazon

37984617R00050